# Agronomy for us all:

# The drive towards a sustainable agricultural future

Tommy Cole

# Table of Content

# Chapter 1

The dawn of agriculture

The great majority of the world's food supply is produced via agriculture, which is the farming-based production of food and products. It has only been extensively accepted for 7,000 years, although having been practiced irregularly over the previous 13,000 years. This is a little period in the lengthy history of humanity as compared to the almost 200,000 years that our predecessors were foraging, hunting, and scavenging in the wild.

In its short existence, agriculture has fundamentally altered human society and supported an expanding global population that has increased from 4 million to 7 billion people since 10,000 BCE.

The path leading up to the present has not been easy. Food supply has sometimes been severely hampered by resource degradation, fast population expansion, sickness, changing climatic conditions, and other factors, with the poor suffering the burden of famine. Along with new and even more dangerous dangers, we nevertheless deal with many of the same problems as our forebears. We might start by studying the past to prepare for an uncertain future.

The oldest fossil evidence of Homo sapiens, anatomically modern humans, is thought to be around 196,000 years old, according to paleoanthropologists. Since the beginning of our species' evolutionary history, humans have gotten most of our food via foraging in the outdoors. The Paleolithic diet was mostly composed of wild plants and fungi, including the wild progenitors of certain species that are now commonly farmed.

Although the ancient hunt for wild animals is sometimes portrayed as an epic battle against woolly mammoths, woolly rhinos, huge elk, and other prehistoric megafauna, early people also learned to forage for simple insects and scavenge the carcasses of deceased animals.

People started gradually moving away from a hunter-gatherer lifestyle toward producing crops and raising animals for sustenance as early as 11,000 BCE. Northern China, Central America, and the Fertile Crescent, an area in the Middle East that gave birth to some of the first civilizations, are among the places in the globe where the transition to agriculture is thought to have happened independently. Most of the agricultural animals that we are used to today had been tamed by 6000 BCE. Except for Australia, all of the main continents had agriculture by 5000 BCE.

Why did humans switch to farming from hunting and gathering? There are several probable explanations, all of which probably had an impact at various points in time and various regions of the world:

It could have been too cold or dry to depend on natural food sources due to climatic changes.
More food may have been needed than could be obtained through foraging in the wild due to higher population density, yet farming nevertheless produced more food per acre even if it took more time and effort.
Woolly mammoths and other megafauna may have gone extinct due to overhunting.
Agriculture would have been a more financially feasible way of living had technology changed, such as tamed seeds.

Historical civilizations

Agriculture, for better or worse, was a major factor in the development of civilizations.

Although farming was likely more labor-intensive than foraging and hunting, it is believed to have produced 10 to 100 times more calories per acre. Denser populations could be supported by more food sources, and farming bound them to their land. Small communities expanded into towns, and those towns expanded into cities.

Agriculture supplied enough food to liberate people from worrying about their daily meals and allow them to pursue other hobbies. People who didn't need to work as farmers became warriors, priests, managers, artists, and intellectuals.

Political and religious leaders emerged to dominate early civilizations as they took form, establishing classes of "haves" and "have-nots." In contrast to hunter-gatherer communities, when resources were often seen as belonging to everyone, agriculture gave rise to a system of land, food, and money ownership that was not (and still is not) fairly divided among the populace.

Some have questioned if eschewing a hunter-gatherer way of life was in the best interests of mankind, citing issues with social inequality, starvation, and armed warfare that emerged after the introduction of farming. In fact, agriculture has been dubbed by one eminent scientist as the "worst mistake in the history of the human race."

That may be true, but it is impractical to go back to a paleolithic way of life given the size and density of the human population today. However, hunting, collecting, and farming may work in conjunction with one another to provide people access to a wider variety of food. For instance, aquatic plants and animals are still harvested from the sea, and even city inhabitants may come upon tasty berries, greens, and mushrooms in their neighborhood parks.

Growth constraints

Agriculture may have enabled civilizations, but it has never served as a barrier to their demise. Throughout history, population expansion, resource depletion, droughts, climatic changes, and other variables that sometimes crippled food supply battled with improvements in agricultural output, with the poor suffering the brunt of hunger.

The land was often cultivated by early farmers in ways that reduced its fertility, much like many of its contemporary equivalents. Technology advancements like irrigation (about 6000 BCE) and the plow (around 3000 BCE) led to significant production improvements, but when used carelessly, they damaged the soil—the fundamental foundation that allows agriculture to take place. Roman farmers had damaged their land to the point that they could no longer produce enough food and were forced to depend on imports from far-off Egypt by the start of the Common Era. One of many cautionary stories about the significance of sustainable agriculture is Rome's inevitable demise.

By 1798, economist Thomas Malthus foresaw worldwide hunger as a result of unbridled population expansion outpacing food supply. This situation has occurred before; from 1300 to 1850, repeated famines spread throughout most of Europe as a result of diminished cropland and shifting temperatures.

Meanwhile, Malthus' detractors contended—and still contend—that scientific progress would prevent hunger by continuously figuring out methods to boost food supply. Malthus' work serves as a reminder that the Earth's potential to sustain human progress is finite, even if his predictions have not come to pass precisely as he predicted.

## THE POPULATION BOOM

The world's population increased from 1.6 billion in 1900 to 7 billion in 2011. Despite this rapid expansion, farmers throughout the globe generated enough calories in 2012 to feed everyone on the planet plus an extra 1.6 billion people. Due to the unequal distribution of those calories across the world's population and the fact that a huge portion of the food produced is never consumed, hunger continues to be a worldwide concern. Even Nevertheless, today's output is enormous compared to prior generations. What has enabled such unheard-of abundance?

So far, improvements in food distribution and production have allowed food supply to keep up with the population increase. Native to the Americas, crops like maize, sweet potatoes, and cassava have spread all over the world.

Over the 18th century, a significant rise in population was supported by the nutrients these abundant crops offered to avoid starvation. The United States became a significant exporter of excess wheat and maize, feeding most of Europe during times of famine abroad thanks to expanded railroads, shipping canals, and improved equipment for storing and transporting food. Farmers were able to transport perishable foods over longer distances because of advancements in refrigerated transport.

Synthetic fertilizers—chemicals produced using a process that converts atmospheric nitrogen into a form that can be applied to crops (ammonia)—are undoubtedly the agricultural advances that have had the greatest impact. Synthetic fertilizers, which were first used in the early 1900s and significantly enhanced crop yields (albeit not without drawbacks), are credited for producing the majority of the world's food throughout the 20th century. Industrial agriculture has made the usage of these and other chemicals a defining characteristic.

# Chapter 2

Modern agriculture

A key source of income is agriculture. Modern irrigation methods, however, have a significant negative influence on the ecosystem. We discuss contemporary agriculture and its effects on the environment in this chapter.

Agriculture is the process of growing plants and keeping domesticated animals (livestock) to provide food, feed, fiber, and many other desirable items. It is the art of controlling plant and animal development for human benefit. Let's investigate the effects of changing agricultural practices on the environment and ecology.

What is modern farming?

To fulfill the world's demands for food, fuel, and fiber, farmers must use less natural resources, such as water, land, and energy, via the use of agricultural advances and modern farming techniques. Other names for contemporary agriculture include agribusiness, intensive farming, organic farming, and sustainable agriculture.

Modern Agriculture and New Agriculture Technology

In contemporary agriculture, innovation is more crucial than ever. The whole sector is confronted with formidable obstacles, including shifting customer desires for transparency and sustainability as well as increased supply-side prices and workforce shortages. Agriculture firms are becoming more and more aware that these problems need quick solutions. Thank goodness agtech, commonly referred to as agricultural technology, has arrived.

The use of technology in farming and agricultural techniques to improve productivity, sustainability, and efficiency in food production is a relatively recent idea. It incorporates a variety of technological disciplines, including automation, biotechnology, smart irrigation, and precision agriculture. In addition, there have been substantial technical developments in fields like blockchain, artificial intelligence, cattle technology, contemporary greenhouse methods, and indoor vertical farming, which we shall cover in more detail in this chapter.

Vertical farming inside

Indoor vertical farming may boost crop yields, make up for a lack of available land, and even lessen the environmental effect of farming by reducing supply chain distance. This novel idea is the technique of growing foods layered one on top of the other in a regulated, enclosed environment. Its main advantage is that, in comparison to conventional farming techniques, it may greatly decrease the amount of area required for plant growth.

The advantage of vertical agriculture is that in certain configurations, plants may thrive without soil. The majority of plants are either hydroponically grown in a bowl of nutrient-rich water or aeroponically grown, where the roots are repeatedly sprayed with water and nutrients.

The benefits of indoor vertical farming are clear, ranging from enhancing agricultural productivity with lower labor costs to promoting sustainable urban expansion. With the help of this innovative agricultural technology, food output may be increased while ensuring predictable harvests by carefully controlling factors like light, humidity, and water year-round.

By deploying robots to manage logistics, planting, and harvesting, farms may overcome the difficulty of the present manpower shortage in the agricultural sector.

Advantages of farming automation

Farm automation, also referred to as "smart farming," is a technology that increases the productivity of farms by automating the cycle of crop or animal production. A growing number of AgTech businesses are focusing on robotics innovation to create robots that can automatically irrigate plants, sow seeds, and operate autonomous tractors and harvesters.

Although these technologies are still relatively new, the sector has witnessed an increase in the number of conventional agricultural businesses incorporating farm automation into their operations since their main objective is to eliminate tedious activities.
technologies used in livestock farming

The traditional livestock sector, which produces essential renewable natural resources that we depend on every day, is undoubtedly the most significant yet underappreciated sector.
Livestock management, sometimes referred to as operating farms, cattle ranches, and other similar agribusinesses, includes keeping precise financial records, managing employees, and guaranteeing the right care and feeding of animals.

However, the world of animal husbandry is changing as a result of agricultural technology breakthroughs. The industry has been tremendously enhanced by these advancements, which have made monitoring and handling cattle simpler and quicker.

The idea of a "connected cow" emerged from the deployment of sensors in herds to track their well-being and boost output. Producers may monitor daily activity and health-related concerns and make operational choices quickly and simply by attaching individual wearable sensors to cows.

The study of an animal's whole gene landscape and how it interacts with other genes to affect the animal's growth and development is known as animal genomics, a new field of agricultural technology. The use of genomics by livestock farmers enables them to assess the genetic risk in their herds and forecast the animal's future profitability. Therefore, producers may maximize the profitability and yields of livestock herds by making strategic choices about the animal selection and breeding of their stock.

Agtech offers the sector significant advantages. The production of cattle herds will increase as a result of data-driven decision-making, which produces better and more effective judgments.

contemporary greenhouses

The greenhouse sector has evolved over the last several decades from modest buildings mostly used for research and aesthetics (such as botanic gardens) to considerably bigger buildings that actively compete with traditional food production on the land. Currently, the total worldwide greenhouse sector generates around $350 billion worth of vegetables yearly, with less than 1% of that output coming from the United States.

Today, the business is seeing a flowering, unlike any other period, in large part because of the enormous recent advances in developing technology. Urban-focused, large-scale greenhouses are starting to appear more often.

The market has undergone significant growth as well as definite trends in recent years. Modern greenhouses are getting more and more technologically advanced, incorporating automated control systems and LED lighting to precisely customize the growth environment. To take advantage of the rising demand for local food, prosperous greenhouse businesses are rapidly expanding and positioning their growing operations close to metropolitan centers.

The greenhouse business is investing more money to achieve these achievements, employing venture capital and other financing sources to set up the necessary infrastructure to compete in the present market.

Technology for precision agriculture

Agriculture is changing, and technology is now a necessary component of any commercial farm. With the use of new precision agriculture firms, farmers will be able to optimize yields by managing every crop-related aspect, including soil moisture, microclimates, and soil conditions. Precision agriculture helps farmers enhance productivity and control expenses by offering more precise methods for planting and producing crops.

Companies that specialize in precision agriculture have great potential to expand. According to a recent study by Grand View Research, Inc., the market for precision agriculture would grow to $43.4 billion by 2025. Farmers of the younger generation are drawn to quicker, more adaptable companies that methodically optimize agricultural output.
Using blockchain to track food

Food fraud, safety recalls, supply chain inefficiencies, and food traceability are all urgent issues in the present food system that may be resolved using blockchain's capacity to monitor owner records and tamper with security. Its distinctive decentralized structure guarantees validated goods and processes, fostering an open market.

Recent talks about food safety have put food traceability at the forefront, especially in light of recent developments in blockchain applications. The perishable nature of food makes the food sector particularly susceptible to errors that might harm human life.

The chain of custody for food must be traceable. Since some parties are still keeping track of information on paper, the present communication architecture within the food ecosystem makes traceability a time-consuming effort. All stakeholders involved in the food value chain may produce and exchange data securely thanks to the blockchain's structure, creating a transparent and responsible system.

Numerous data points with proprietary labels may be promptly and unalterably captured. As a consequence, it is possible to keep track of food movement in real-time from farm to table.

Blockchain in the food industry has applications beyond only assuring food safety.

By creating a ledger in the network and balancing market prices, it also provides value to the present market. Instead of using data from the full value chain, the conventional pricing mechanism for buying and selling depends on the opinions of the parties involved. Giving people access to data would result in a very transparent market with a comprehensive picture of supply and demand.

Artificial intelligence and farming

These can keep an eye on things like soil quality, plant health, temperature, humidity, and more. The goal is to use cutting-edge technology that can tell farmers more than the human eye can see to help them grasp what's occurring on the ground. Additionally, it is quicker in addition to being more precise.

Algorithms using remote sensors translate field perimeters into statistical information that farmers can comprehend and utilize to guide their decisions. Data processing algorithms adjust and learn as a result of the data they receive.

The algorithm's ability to forecast various outcomes improves with more inputs and data collection. The objective is to provide farmers with the tools they need to utilize artificial intelligence to make better choices in the field and ultimately produce better crops.

Environmental effects of modern agriculture

As is well known, modern agriculture has made food more accessible and affordable while also increasing food production, sustainability, and the production of biofuels. However, since it is based on a high input-high output technology that uses hybrid seeds of high-yielding varieties together with copious amounts of irrigation water, fertilizer, and pesticides, it also contributes to environmental issues. The following is a discussion of how modern agriculture affects the environment:

Earth Erosion

Due to the overabundance of water, cropland loses its top layer of rich soil. As a result, nutrient-rich soil that hindered production is lost. Additionally, it contributes to global warming because soil carbon is released from particle organic matter in water bodies due to silt.

Water contamination in the earth

One of the major sources of water for irrigation is groundwater. Nitrogenous fertilizers from agricultural areas eventually pollute groundwater after leaching into the soil. The "Blue Baby Syndrome" is a major health risk that predominantly affects babies and may potentially be fatal when the nitrate content of groundwater surpasses 25 mg/l.

salinity and standing water

Due to poor farm drainage management, one of the causes of low production is the salt of the soil. As a result of the plant's roots not receiving enough oxygen to breathe in this scenario, the crop yield and mechanical strength are both poor.

Eutrophication

It describes the addition of synthetic or natural materials, such as nitrates and phosphate, to a freshwater system via fertilizers or sewage. It causes the phytoplankton to "bloom," or improve the water body's primary production.

The phenomena of eutrophication (EU = more, eutrophication = nutrition) is brought on by an over-nourishment of lakes and other bodies of water caused by the excessive use of fertilizers that include nitrogen and phosphorus.

excessive pesticide usage

Numerous insecticides are used to eradicate pests and increase agricultural yields. In the past, bugs were killed with arsenic, sulfur, lead, and mercury. For instance, insecticides like Dichloro Diphenyl Trichloroethane (DDT) were utilized, but sadly they also affected beneficial pests. The fact that many pesticides are non-biodegradable and connected to food chains that are detrimental to people is essential.

Since the start of industrialization, agriculture's relative importance has decreased progressively, and in 2006, the services sector surpassed agriculture as the economic sector with the most people employed globally for the first time in history. But we fail to recognize the need for agriculture if we are to continue existing.

# Chapter 3

Classification of agronomic plants

The main agronomic crops are categorized based on how they are used. In this sense, the following categories might be applied to the crops:

1. Cereal crops, commonly referred to as grain crops

These grasses are raised for their palatable seeds. Wheat, rice, maize, barley, oats, sorghum, millet, and other crops are examples.

2. Forage Plants

These are the crops that are grown for grazing by animals or green chop, hay, silage, or soiling. These crops have fiber levels that are above 25% of dry matter. Like clovers and grasses, forage crops are members of the Leguminosae and Graminae families.

Sorghum, maize, and other coarse crops are referred to as fodder crops because they can be collected whole and fed to animals.

## 3. Crops of Oilseed

These plants were grown especially to have their seeds used for oil extraction. For instance, flax, linseed, sunflower, safflower, sesame, castor bean, mustard, rapeseed, canola, and so on.

## 4. Fiber Plants

These plants are specifically cultivated to harvest the fiber. Clothes, ropes, bags, and other items are made using this material. For instance, cotton, jute, flax, sunkukra, kenaf, and sun hemp.

## 5. Sugar Cane

The juice obtained from these plants is used to make edible sugar. For instance, sweet sorghum, sugar beets, and sugar cane.

6. Pulses or Crops for Grain

These members of the Leguminosae family are grown for their delicious seeds. For instance, pigeon peas, cowpeas, lima beans, mung beans, and mash beans.

7. Crops of Root and Tuber

These crops, including rhizomes, bulbs, tubers, corms, and stem tubers, are farmed for their subterranean economic components. For instance, turnip, radish, carrot, potato, groundnut, onion, and garlic.

8. Garden or Vegetable Crops

crops that are raised for their tasty seeds, leaves, and shoots. Examples include cucumber, broccoli, asparagus, cauliflower, spinach, squash, pumpkin, tomato, eggplant, okra, and garden peas.

9. Condiment Crops

Mint, chilies, and coriander are all grown for use as seasonings.

10. Drug or Narcotic Crops

The crops that are used as narcotic or drug crops include tobacco, poppy, tea, coffee, and peppermint.

# Chapter 4

Classification of nutritional plants

A significant portion of human nutrition and health comes from plant-based diets. The two primary types of nutrition for humans are macronutrients and micronutrients. Macronutrient balance and a reliable supply of micronutrients are essential for sustaining healthy health.

On processed, labeled items at the grocery store, it is often simple to obtain information on the number of nutrients in a product. However, it is often absent from meals that are bulked up and fresh, such as grains, vegetables, and fruits.

Human nutrition is based on our need to get adequate minerals and vitamins to operate as well as our need to obtain our energy from food. The macronutrients in our diet, particularly carbs, and fats, provide us with the majority of our energy (or calories).

Although protein may also provide us with energy, it is preferable for us to utilize it as a source of amino acids so that our bodies can produce protein. Additionally, some various crops and macronutrients might be healthier or worse for you, as well as various kinds of fats, proteins, and carbs.

1. Carbohydrates

Plants produce three different kinds of carbohydrates: sugars, starches, and fiber. We need a constant supply of sugar in our bodies because it powers our metabolism. The three primary sugar-producing crops are maize, sugar beets, and sugar cane.

Typically, these crops need processing to separate the sugar from the plant material. While sugar is necessary for energy and nourishment, we are aware that consuming too much of it per serving is unhealthy. Blood sugar increases brought on by an excessive amount of sugar in our meals may eventually result in diabetes.

Therefore, adding starch—another kind of carbohydrate—to the diet is a smart idea. Long sugar chains make up the structure of starches. This implies that before we can use the starches as fuel, our bodies must struggle to break them down. This 'job' is beneficial! The blood sugar rise decreases as the body works harder at it. Green peas and cowpeas, as well as the legume crops rice, wheat, maize, oats, barley, sorghum, and millet, are all excellent suppliers of starch.

A food with excellent starch is a plantain. Some root and tuber crops, including potatoes, sweet potatoes, yams, cassava, and parsnips, store their starch below the soil.

2. Fibers

During their metabolic processes, plants also convert carbohydrates into fibers. However, the body struggles to break down fiber and assimilate the underlying carbs for energy. Instead, the health of the gut depends on fiber. Although we don't need the microorganisms in our stomach for energy, they do, and they too must be maintained healthy!

Additionally, microorganisms may break down certain fibers before our body can utilize the carbohydrate for energy. Vegetables, fruits, and whole-grain cereals all contain fiber. The greatest thing to do is to change it up with our diets since there are so many various sorts and they are all crucial to the diet.

3. Fats

Because eating too many carbohydrates is unhealthy, it's crucial to balance our requirement for fat with our consumption of carbohydrates. This fat may be extracted from the plant itself or transformed into culinary oils. Peanuts, soybean, canola, sunflower, and coconut are the most significant crops for the production of cooking oils.

Like carbs, various crops may produce different types of fats. As an example, healthy sources of unsaturated fats (the "better-for-you" fats) include tree nuts, peanuts, canola, and avocado.

4. Protein

The primary source of the amino acids we need to be healthy is dietary protein. Although we often associate protein with animal goods, plants can also produce it. However, since certain plants may be deficient in specific kinds of amino acids, they are regarded as having "incomplete" protein.

For instance, certain legumes and cereals may be deficient in methionine or lysine, respectively. As a result, it's critical to balance plant proteins from various crops. Beans, lentils, soybeans, green peas, cowpeas, quinoa, and peanuts are all excellent sources of plant protein. There are proteins in the seeds of other cereal crops as well, but they are more crucial for the quality of baked goods than for human nourishment.

5. Micronutrients

In contrast to macronutrients, which provide us with energy, micronutrients help our bodies run smoothly. Vitamins and minerals are the two categories of micronutrients. It's less about balancing the sorts of micronutrients and more about making sure we get enough of both since there is a specific quantity needed for each of them for us to be in good health.

While whole grain cereals, legumes, roots, and tubers are also rich sources of vitamins and minerals in addition to fruits and vegetables, fruits and vegetables are the best. For instance, potatoes are abundant in potassium, beans often contain a lot of iron, and processed vegetable oils, as mentioned above, sometimes include a lot of vitamin E.

The most crucial aspect of nutrition is balanced since getting too much of one vitamin typically means getting too little of another. Different plants generate various forms of protein, lipids, carbs, vitamins, and minerals. This is why it is beneficial to the body's health to include a variety of food crops in the diet.

# Chapter 5

What to grow for medicine

You may utilize freshly picked herbs in your cooking if you grow herbs in your garden. Anyone who has used them for cooking would attest to the fact that they are much superior to dried or pre-packaged herbs. Every plant also has healing qualities. They are used in conventional medicine to treat common health issues such as the common cold, fever, burns, cuts, and wounds.

Natural ingredients found in herbal plants have been utilized for treating ailments for millennia. They are often used in herbal treatments and cuisine. Compared to manufactured or pharmaceutical treatments, herbal medications are thought to be safer. These plants or their crude medicines are used to make the majority of contemporary medication.

Several medicinal plants may improve health and aid in sickness prevention. Some even serve as nutritional supplements. You may save time and money by growing some of these plants at home. Ashwagandha plant, Allium sativum, Vitex negundo, stinging nettle, orange blossoms, chamomile flowers, and others are examples of herbal plants having therapeutic characteristics.

Here are 10 of our favorite home-grown therapeutic herbs.

1. Aloe vera

The earliest known medicinal plant in the world is probably aloe vera. Around 4000 BC, the ancient Egyptians made the first discovery of it. Aloe was thought to have healing powers. Hippocrates (460 BC–370 BC) later suggested aloe as a wound cure. Arab doctors treated eye conditions using aloe in medieval times. Aloe gained popularity among Europeans throughout the 16th century as a result of its capacity to treat burns.

Aloe is now often utilized in cosmetic products. Aloe vera gel made from the plant's leaves is used to treat bacterial infections, skin irritation, small wounds, sunburns, and other skin disorders. It is furthermore used to treat sports injuries, muscular spasms, sprains, and arthritis-related edema. Aloe vera gel is further used to decrease scarring after surgery.

Aloe vera plants have high vitamin C content in their leaves, which helps them fight off cold sores. Polysaccharides in the gel may enhance blood circulation. These substances promote cell development as well. Antioxidant qualities in aloe vera plant extract save cells from harm. Additionally, it possesses antibacterial qualities.

Aloe vera comes in a variety of varieties. Aloe barbadensis is the most prevalent kind.

2. Lemon grass

Tropical conditions are ideal for growing the plant lemongrass. It is indigenous to Sri Lanka and India. Dr. John Witherspoon brought it to Florida in 1857. He sowed seeds close to his house after returning from his trip to India. They flourished, so he started selling them at neighborhood markets.

Medicine is made from both the leaves and the oil. To treat digestive system spasms, gastric ulcers, high blood pressure, constipation, diarrhea, flatulence, heartburn, dyspepsia, indigestion, nausea, vomiting, anxiety, rheumatic pains, sore throats, and toothaches, the oil is extracted from the leaves. The oil is also used as a mild astringent and to destroy bacteria.

Tea made with lemongrass eases uncomfortable menstrual cramps and stomach aches. It has a calming and tranquil impact.

Lemongrass comes in two different kinds. Lemongrass comes in two varieties: "wild" lemongrass and "domestic" lemongrass. All around Asia, you may find wild lemongrass growing. Commercial lemongrass cultivation is practiced in Hawaii, Australia, New Zealand, Malaysia, Thailand, and Indonesia.

3. Fenugreek

Fenugreek has been used as a medicine for a very long time. Fenugreek seeds have been used as a dietary supplement and even a medication by the ancient Egyptians. They thought that fenugreek enhanced digestion and increased vigor.

The Greeks and Romans employed fenugreek for its medicinal properties in ancient times. Fenugreek is still utilized today for its medical benefits all over the world.

Diosgenin is fenugreek's primary active component. Fenugreek contains the steroidal saponin diosgenin. Natural substances called saponins function as detergents. They eliminate toxins and waste products as well as other undesirable items from the body.

Diosgenin is often used to treat diabetes since it helps to manage insulin. Additionally, it raises testosterone levels and supports hormone balance.

Constipation may also be treated with fenugreek. Fenugreek stimulates the digestive tract and boosts bile flow when taken orally. The liver produces bile, a liquid that helps break down fats and other nutrients. It promotes continued digestive health.

Breast cancer may also be treated with fenugreek. According to research, fenugreek includes compounds that aid in slowing the development of tumors and have anti-cancer qualities. The presence of diosgenin, which contains estrogenic action, maybe the cause of this effect. The usage of fenugreek to treat high cholesterol may be due to its capacity to suppress the formation of tumors. According to studies, fenugreek may lower overall cholesterol levels by as much as 20%.

For women who are expecting or breastfeeding, fenugreek may also be beneficial. Fenugreek encourages lactation and boosts milk output. Additionally, it could aid in reducing morning sickness.

Fenugreek has a variety of applications, however not everyone should use it. This herb should not be used by persons who have gallbladder issues, are taking medicine for heart disease, or are allergic to fenugreek.

## 4. Rosemary

Humans have utilized rosemary for a variety of reasons throughout history. We still utilize rosemary now for its therapeutic properties and applications. certain of the most popular applications include lowering stress, enhancing cognitive function, promoting hair development, assisting in pain relief, deterring certain insects, boosting circulation, and reducing joint inflammation. The oil is utilized in aromatherapy since the plant is fragrant.

The plant species of rosemary are many. The "common" rosemary plant is one kind of herb. The main reason common rosemary is produced is for use in cooking. The "garden" kind of rosemary is a different variety. Garden rosemary is far more difficult to grow than ordinary rosemary and is often seen growing wild.

One further name for rosemary is the "herb of remembrance." Because of this, it is often connected to Christmas. People feel that rosemary improves their holiday memory.

5. Cinnamon

Digestive health may be enhanced by peppermint. It includes menthol, which promotes the secretion of digestive fluids and assists in nutritional absorption.

Your breath may smell better and your dental health may be improved by peppermint. Additionally, it aids with focus. Menthol is proven to improve oral blood flow and lessen foul breath.

Peppermint helps with allergies and contains antimicrobial effects. Inflammation is reduced and microorganisms are killed by menthol.

Congestion and headache relief is provided by peppermint.

Treatments for indigestion, diarrhea, nausea, and vomiting include peppermint oil.

Peppermint is simple to cultivate at home and has several therapeutic uses.

6. Thyme

Thyme has a wide range of applications and advantages. Among them are: - aids in the treatment of acne - reduces blood pressure - increases immunity - purifies - deters pests - aromatherapy - elevates mood.

7. Lavender

Beautiful lavender blooms wonderfully both inside and outdoors. It has gorgeous blossoms and has a strong fragrance. Landscapes and gardens often include lavender plants. Many individuals take pleasure in cultivating lavender in their own homes. Lavender is low maintenance and simple to care for.

The advantages of cultivating lavender at home are many. Any garden or landscape would benefit from the addition of lavender. It is simple to cultivate and needs little sunshine or water. It requires little upkeep and simply sporadic watering. Lavender has a strong aroma and looks beautiful in any space. A significant aromatic plant, it.

Lavender offers a lot of advantages. It could help with mental disorders, promote sleep, ease menstrual cramps, and enhance skin health. Lavender is often used as an aromatherapy ingredient and dietary supplement to treat tiredness, anxiety, and depression.

Growing lavender at home is simple.

8. Tulsi

According to research, the benefits of tulsi include a natural immunity booster; analgesic properties that reduce pain and fever; analgesic properties that reduce stress and blood pressure; analgesic properties that reduce cold, cough, and other respiratory disorders; anti-cancer properties that are good for heart health and diabetes patients; and benefits for kidney stones and gouty arthritis.

There are several medical uses for tulsi. Tulsi may be grown in gardens or on balconies. In India, tulsi is revered as the herb's queen.

It is one of the herbs that are most often planted in gardens.

9. Ginger

Many health advantages of ginger exist. The treatment of nausea, decreasing blood sugar levels, assisting with arthritis, and reducing heart disease risk factors are a few of the medicinal advantages. However, it could also aid in lowering cholesterol and weight reduction.

Ginger may also aid in the recovery from the flu and cold. Even morning sickness during pregnancy could be helped by it.

10. The curry leaf

Curry leaves are utilized in both Ayurvedic medicine and cookery. They have a reputation for treating digestive issues such as gastritis, indigestion, acid reflux, and ulcers. Along with treating respiratory ailments including bronchitis and urinary tract infections, they are also used to treat diabetes, liver illnesses, cold symptoms, coughs, asthma, fevers, malaria, rheumatism, and gout.

Curry leaves are regarded as one of the "Holy Trinity" of South Indian tastes in India. They are used to make stews, soups, and curries.

# Chapter 6

Beware of these toxic plants

Plants may seem to be innocent enough, yet they may contain some of the most lethal toxins ever discovered. Poisonous plants have caused human fatalities throughout history, from Socrates' death from poison hemlock to children's unintentional use of deadly nightshade. With the help of this macabre list, you may learn about some of the most notorious plants and their poisons.

## 1. (Cicuta maculata) Water Hemlock

The plant known for killing Socrates, poison hemlock, is linked to water hemlock, which has been called "the most violently toxic plant in North America." Water hemlock is a large wildflower in the carrot family that resembles Queen Anne's lace and is sometimes mistaken for edible celery or parsnips.

However, water hemlock is loaded with lethal cicutoxin, particularly in the roots, and anybody unlucky enough to ingest it would quickly experience possibly fatal symptoms. Amnesia or persistent tremors are often experienced by persons who survive painful convulsions, stomach pains, sickness, and death.

## 2. (Atropa belladonna) Deadly Nightshade

The Danes were allegedly poisoned by Macbeth's warriors using wine concocted from the delicious fruit of the poisonous nightshade. The berries' deliciousness is what often tempts kids and unaware adults to devour this deadly plant. Deadly nightshade is a plant that is indigenous to woodland or waste regions in central and southern Eurasia.

It has dull green leaves and lustrous, black berries the size of cherries. Nightshade paralyzes the body's involuntary muscles, including the heart, by containing atropine and scopolamine in its stems, leaves, berries, and roots. Even direct physical touch with the leaves might irritate the skin.

## 3. (Ageratina altissima) White Snakeroot

Nancy Hanks, the mother of Abraham Lincoln, perished at the hands of a harmless herb called white snakeroot. The North American plant known as "white snakeroot" has flat-topped clusters of tiny white blooms and is poisonous because it contains trematol. Poor Nancy Hanks was poisoned by only consuming the milk of a cow that had grazed on the plant, unlike many who have passed away by directly swallowing lethal plants.

Poisoned cattle may spread the toxin to humans via their flesh and milk. Loss of appetite, nausea, weakness, stomach pain, a reddish tongue, abnormal blood acidity, and mortality are all signs of "milk poisoning." Fortunately, farmers are taking steps to remove the plant from animal pastures now that they are aware of this potentially fatal risk.

4. Ricinius communis, the castor bean

The castor bean, a beautiful plant indigenous to Africa, is often cultivated as an ornamental. Castor oil is made from processed seeds, which also happen to naturally contain the toxin ricin, which is lethal in tiny doses. A youngster may be killed in as few as one or two seeds, and an adult in as many as eight.

Ricin may result in severe vomiting, diarrhea, convulsions, and even death. It does this by preventing the creation of proteins inside cells. Georgi Markov, a journalist who spoke out against the Bulgarian government, was killed with poison in 1978. It has also been used to send poison to various American politicians in foiled terrorist attacks. Accidental ingestion by children and animals causes the majority of deaths.

## 5. (Abrus precatorius) Rosary Pea

These pompously titled seeds, sometimes known as jequirity beans, contain abrin, a very lethal ribosome-inhibiting protein. Native to tropical regions, rosary peas are often utilized in jewelry and prayer rosaries.

Despite not being toxic when whole, seeds that have been bitten, cracked, or scraped may be fatal. It is reported that many jewelry makers have become sick or passed away after unintentionally pricking their fingers while working with the seeds since it only takes 3 micrograms of abrin to kill an adult, which is less poison than is present in a single seed.

Abrin, like ricin, stops cells from making proteins and may lead to organ failure in four days.

6. Nerium oleander, or oleander

Oleander is a stunning shrub with spectacular blossoms that was first mentioned by Pliny the Elder in Ancient Rome. Despite being often cultivated as a hedge and ornamental, oleander plants are poisonous and contain the fatal cardiac glycosides oleandrin and neriine in all of their components.

Oleander sap is known to irritate certain people's skin, and eating it may result in vomiting, diarrhea, an irregular heartbeat, seizures, coma, and death. The oleander's poisons are so potent that ingesting honey produced by bees that visited the blossoms rendered some humans sick. Fortunately, oleander poisoning seldom results in death since the plant is very unpleasant and rapidly dissuades people from trying any of the plants.

7. Nicotiana tabacum, or tobacco

The most frequently used commercial non-food plant in the world is tobacco. Nicotine and anabasine, two poisonous alkaloids present in all parts of the plant but particularly the leaves, may be lethal if consumed. Despite being classified as a heart toxin, nicotine from tobacco is both psychotropic and addictive and is extensively eaten worldwide. More than 5 million people die each year from tobacco usage, making it perhaps the world's deadliest plant.

# Chapter 7

The anatomy of plants

Plant tissues and cells are studied to better understand how these creatures are put together and function. These investigations are crucial because they help us learn how to take care of plants and combat plant illnesses. Phytotomy is another name for plant anatomy.

A plant is a complicated structure made up of several elements that together make up the whole plant. Knowing the names of each component can help you comprehend how the plant functions a whole lot better. Since there is often a correlation between the location of an essential oil in a plant and its therapeutic function, this might be useful for aromatherapists who need to know what portion of the plant an essential oil was extracted from.

Everyone may better appreciate the craft of distillation and extraction by having a basic understanding of plant anatomy.

The length of a plant's life

Plant species differ not only in terms of appearance but also in terms of lifespan. Biennial plants produce just leaves the first year and flowers the second, whereas annual blooming plants only survive for one year.

Long-lived perennial plants may last for over two years. They may be deciduous (lose their leaves in the fall) or evergreen (never lose their leaves). The geographical location and cultural goal of a plant may affect whether it is classified as an annual, biennial, or perennial. These several biological lifecycles are all used to extract essential oils.

All plants are made up of the following fundamental components.

1. The flowers

Although not all plants bloom, many of the ones used to make essential oils do, such as lavender (Lavandula angustifolia), roses (Rosa damascena), and rosemary (Rosmarinus officinalis).

A plant's blossom is a sophisticated structure. The petals of a flower are made up of the corolla. The calyx is made up of the outer, or green, leaves. The stamen contains the pollen that attracts insects and birds. The pistil is made up of the ovary, the style, and the stigma of the flower.

The Seeds and Fruits

A plant's nucleus is found in the seed, and if the appropriate circumstances exist for growth, the seed may produce a new plant. Fruits on plants may be categorized in one of the ways listed below:

Folliculate legume
drupe achenium caryopsis cremocarp
nut berry samara pome pepo silique capsule
cone
Lemon (Citrus limon) and sweet orange
(Citrus sinensis) are examples of plants with
fruits that may be used to make essential
oils.

## 2. The Leaf

The petiole, a portion of the stalk, is where
the leaves develop. The forms, textures, and
colors of leaves may be short, plump, long,
thin, hairy, curved, indented, wispy, or any
other combination of these. Botanically
speaking, a plant's many leaf kinds are
classified as follows:

Lanceolate Cuneiform
Sagittate
Ovate Cordate
Pinnate Pectinate Runcinate Lyrate

Palmate Pedate Obovate
Reniform
Hastate Serrate Peltate
Dentate
Crenate Sinuate

Cinnamomum zeylanicum and citrus aurantium var. amara, often known as cinnamon and petitgrain, are plants that generate an essential oil from their leaves.

3. The Stem

All blooming plants have stems, which are drawn out from the base and toward the light and air. Some plants may seem to have no stems, yet they fact contain a stem that is either very short or underground. The trunk of a tree is its main structural component.

Herbs have stalks that fall off when they blossom. All of these plant species are used for the extraction of essential oils.

Although clove (Syzygium aromaticum) generates an essential oil from the stem, aromatherapists always prefer to utilize clove bud oil since it is far less irritating to the skin.

## 4. The Roots

A plant's root is often found in the soil underneath it. It serves as the plant's anchor. Root types include:

Fusiform roots have roots that taper up and down, like radish (Rhapanus sativus) roots.
Fasciculated root: thickened fibers or branches
In a tuberiferous root (Solanum tuberosum), some of the root's branches develop into rounded knobs and sometimes end in a branch known as a palmate root.

Aerial root: When a plant extends roots into the open air, as in the case of Indian corn,

Conical root: A carrot (Daucus carota) is an example of a plant with a root that consistently tapers from the crown to the plant's apex.

As in the case of a turnip (Brassica napa), a napiform root is inflated at the base and extends more horizontally than vertically.

The thick, spreading root seen in plants like ginger (Zingiber officinale) is known as a rhizome.

The roots of the ginger plant (Zingiber officinale) provide an essential oil.

# Chapter 8

Genetic modification of plants

Foods that have undergone genetic engineering (GE) have had their DNA altered using genes from other plants or animals. The desired trait's gene from one plant or animal is taken by scientists and put into the cell of another plant or animal.

Function

Bacteria, other very tiny creatures, plants, and animals may all be genetically modified. Scientists may transfer desirable genes from one plant or animal to another via genetic engineering. Likewise, genes may be transferred from an animal to a plant or the opposite. GMOs, or genetically modified organisms, are another term for this.

Selective breeding is not the same as the procedure used to make GE foods. Breeding plants that have the required features is a part of this process. This eventually produces progeny with those desirable features.

Selective breeding may sometimes produce undesirable features, which is one of its drawbacks. One particular gene may be inserted via genetic engineering. By doing this, additional genes carrying undesirable features are avoided. Using genetic engineering may hasten the process of developing novel foods with desired properties.

The following are potential advantages of genetic engineering:

higher-quality food
better food
Plants that are resistant to disease and drought and use less environmental resources (such as water and fertilizer)
Using fewer insecticides

increased food supply with lower prices and a longer shelf life
faster-growing animals and vegetation
Food with better qualities, such as potatoes that fry with less of a chemical that causes cancer
foods used in medicine that might be utilized as vaccinations or other treatments

Concerns pertaining GE foods that have been voiced out include:

food production that might result in an allergic or harmful response
Unexpected or detrimental genetic alterations
accidentally transferring genes from one genetically modified plant or animal to another that wasn't supposed to be modified
foods with fewer nutritional benefits

Food Sources

The list of food sources has grown.

The principal GE crops cultivated in the US are cotton, corn, and soybeans. The majority of these are used to create foodstuffs like:

Corn syrup is a common sweetener for meals and beverages.
soups and sauces include corn starch.
Snack foods, breads, salad dressings, and mayonnaise are all made using soy, maize, and canola oils.
Beet sugar, or simple sugar
Animal feed

Some more significant GE crops are:

Collapse Apples Papayas Potatoes Squash Side Effects The Side Effects section has been enlarged.
Consuming GE foods has no negative consequences.

Recommendations.

The National Academy of Science, the World Health Organization, and several other significant scientific bodies from across the world have examined the studies on GE foods and have not discovered any proof that they are dangerous. There have been no reports of GE food-related illnesses, accidents, or environmental damage. meals made using genetic engineering are as safe as natural meals.

Food makers are now required by the US Department of Agriculture to provide information regarding bioengineered foods and their components.

# Chapter 9

Global concerns about food production

The historic agreements that were made during the Rio de Janeiro Earth Summit in 1992 to direct sustainable development throughout the globe made it notable. Human beings are at the forefront of concern for sustainable development, according to the first principle of the 1992 Rio Declaration on Environment and Development.

They have the right to live a productive, healthy life in harmony with the environment. Twenty years later, we still haven't achieved this essential goal: too many people still don't live productive, healthy lives in balance with the environment.

There are over 925 million hungry individuals worldwide. If one in every seven people is left behind, we cannot refer to progress as sustainable. Hunger also exists, which is absurd given that the globe currently produces enough food to feed everyone. Hundreds of millions more people have obesity-related illnesses.

It follows that the Rio+20 discussion must focus on ending hunger and enhancing human nutrition. The push for the world to feed itself more sustainably and fairly may and should come from the impending United Nations Conference on Sustainable Development.

The realization that the majority of the world's poor and food insecure people, about 75% of whom reside in rural regions, rely primarily on agricultural systems—which include non-food and food items, livestock, fisheries, and forestry—must be the starting point. The vast majority of earth's natural resource managers are the billions of individuals who oversee agricultural systems, ranging from the very poor to commercial farmers.

Because of its contributions on the environmental, economic, and social fronts, agriculture is thus crucial to finding a sustainable solution. The lives and health of people may be improved, and healthier ecosystems can result from better agricultural and food systems. With its focus on a small variety of crops and high reliance on chemicals, energy, and capital, the dominant agricultural model we inherited from the Green Revolution of the 1960s is unable to handle the challenges of the new century.

Between 1960 and 2000, cereal output increased, albeit at a significant expense. Land degradation and deforestation, excessive groundwater extraction, greenhouse gas emissions, loss of biodiversity, and nitrate poisoning of water systems are examples of collateral harm.

Agriculture is not only one of the industries most impacted by climate change, which separates farmers—mostly small-scale ones—from historically agricultural territories, but it also has an impact on the environment and contributes to it.

The Food and Agriculture Organization (FAO) has calculated that by 2050, we would need to produce 60% more food to feed a global population of 9.3 billion people. A farming-as-usual strategy would put too much strain on our natural resources to do that. We must thus start a movement toward a greener world. By using a variety of methods that are more in tune with ecosystems, minimizing the use of external inputs, and assisting farmers in coping with the increasingly frequent weather extremes brought on by climate change, we can sustainably increase crop production while also lowering greenhouse gas emissions.

Small-scale farmers may benefit from and have access to this kind of farming because it is tailored to their needs, places a focus on regional crop types, and uses traditional knowledge to support natural ecosystem processes rather than fighting them.

At the same time, we must promote increased environmental consciousness among industrial-scale, intensive farmers. This may be achieved by offering the appropriate rewards for sustainable behaviors and sanctions for those that are not.

There is no question that by 2050, we will be able to produce 60% more food. Nevertheless, we shouldn't assume that the 60% figure is a given. We must find methods to feed the globe with fewer resources.

The fact is that we wastefully produce, handle, distribute, and consume our food. Around 1.3 billion tonnes, or about one-third, of the food produced for human consumption worldwide each year is lost or squandered. Approximately the same amount of food is wasted in industrialized and developing nations, 670 and 630 million tonnes, respectively.

The majority of food losses take place in underdeveloped nations, however, this may be changed by boosting infrastructure investments and production, harvest, storage, post-harvest, and processing expenditures.

Food wastage is a concern, especially in developed nations where customers and merchants discard perfectly edible meals. In Europe and North America, consumers generate between 95 and 115 kg of garbage per person per year. Consumers in South and Southeast Asia and sub-Saharan Africa only discard 6 to 11 kg of food each year.

We would no longer need to produce 60% more food if we could save some of the food we now throw away. We would have enough food to feed an extra 500 million people annually if we could cut food loss and waste by around only 25%. The public's health and the environment would both gain greatly from a shift to healthier, more environmentally friendly diets.

Nine billion people cannot be fed a diet high in animal protein in 2050. A kilogram of grain requires 1,500 liters of water, but a kilogram of meat needs 15,000 liters. Better diets can help relieve the strain on our natural resources and address the obesity issue, which is an increasing global concern.

Nevertheless, supplying enough food to feed everyone on the planet does not provide food security. Despite having adequate food for everyone, there is still hunger today. By 2050, agricultural production might grow by 60%, but 300 million people will still lack adequate access to food, making them food insecure. The key to hunger is access. Most often, inadequate nutrition is caused by people's inability to produce enough food for themselves or their lack of financial resources to do so.

It's critical to take action against hunger on a global scale, but we also need to have a strong local impact since that's where people eat and live. They don't buy food at international marketplaces. Rural regions are home to more than 70% of the world's poor, therefore improving their standard of living would go a long way toward achieving global food security. They can sustain themselves and provide food for nearby markets if they produce.

To better organize themselves and get access to possibilities, farmer groups, and cooperatives might benefit from being strengthened.

Small-scale farming is one novel strategy that is increasingly being employed in conjunction with cash transfers and pay-for-work programs. In this approach, low-income households may purchase food from local farms. Additionally, it provides a financial boost to small rural communities' economies, assisting in the beginning of a positive feedback loop where individuals who were not previously customers contribute to future expansion.

Linking small-scale manufacturing with food procurement programs like school lunches is a win-win approach. These programs shift the focus away from the conventional emphasis on technology transfer and food assistance and provide a fresh viewpoint on rural development and food interventions.

To put us on a route toward sustainable development, where the goal of food and nutrition security and a transformed farm and food system plays a prominent role, Rio+20 must result in transformative shifts of attitudes, priorities, policies, and investments. This is a mission that is considerably greater than FAO, the UN organizations with offices in Rome, or the UN as a whole. We must all work together to create a more sustainable and secure food future via a discourse including governments, commercial companies, civil society groups, and other parties.

We must investigate the intersection of sustainability, climate change, and food security agendas because it is essential to a healthy future. Rio+20 gives us the chance to achieve that. We cannot allow it to escape our grasp.

The UN Chronicle is not a legally binding document. It is an honor to welcome top

United Nations officials as well as eminent speakers from outside the UN system whose opinions may not necessarily reflect those of the UN.

Similarly, the lines and names shown, as well as the designations used, in maps or publications do not automatically indicate United Nations approval or support.

What Consequences Will the World Population Pass 8 Billion Have for Sustainability and Planetary Health?

The social, demographic, economic, and environmental decisions we make will, in the end, determine the viability of our economic system and the health of the planet. Each of these factors is significant and has the potential to either exacerbate or lessen the effects of the others.

Healthy Forests Are Essential for Sustainable Development and Human Health
The international community, and national governments in particular, need to embrace a multidimensional "One Health" strategy that sees the interconnectedness and codependence of human, plant, and animal health.

# Chapter 10

How to Sustainably Feed the population in coming times

The quantity of food we now produce falls well short of what will be required to feed everyone by 2050. By 2050, there will be around 10 billion people on Earth, which means there will be almost 3 billion more people to feed than there were in 2010.

People will eat more animal-based, resource-intensive diets as earnings grow. At the same time, we must cease converting the few remaining forests into agricultural land and drastically reduce greenhouse gas (GHG) emissions from agricultural activities. Here are actions to take:

1. Reduce food loss and waste

25% of the food that is produced for human use is wasted. Losses and waste happen at every step of the food chain, from farm to table. By 2050, the food gap would be closed by 12%, the land gap would be closed by 27%, and the GHG mitigation gap would be closed by 15% if food loss and waste were reduced by 25%.

Measuring food waste, establishing reduction goals, enhancing food storage in poor nations, and simplifying expiry labeling are all necessary actions.

2. Change to sustainable, healthier diets.

Between 2010 and 2050, more ruminant meat (beef, lamb, and goat) is expected to be consumed. The most widely eaten ruminant meat, beef, requires a lot of resources to grow; it takes up 20 times as much land and emits 20 times as much greenhouse gas (GHG) per gram of digestible protein as typical plant proteins like beans, peas, and lentils.

By 2050, cutting the daily calorie intake of ruminant meat to 52, or about 1.5 hamburgers per week, would cut the gap in GHG mitigation in half and close the land gap. This would mean cutting down on beef and lamb consumption by almost half in North America. The marketing of plant-based meals has to be improved, meat replacements need to be improved, and regulations that encourage the consumption of plant-based foods need to be implemented.

3. Prevent bioenergy from undercutting food crops and agricultural land.

The gaps in food, land, and GHG mitigation would worsen if bioenergy uses crops that compete with food production, such as energy or food crops, or dedicated land. Using all the biomass that was collected in the year 2000—including crops, agricultural byproducts, grass used by cattle, and wood—would only provide around 20% of the world's energy demands in 2050.

The food gap would drop from 56 to 49 percent if current biofuel production in agricultural areas were phased out. Eliminating biofuel subsidies and not recognizing bioenergy as "carbon-neutral" in renewable energy regulations and GHG trading programs are two actions that need to be taken.

4. Achieve fertility rates equivalent to replacement.

The demographic gap is mostly caused by population increase, of which one-third is predicted in Asia and half in Africa. By 2050, the majority of the globe will have replacement fertility (2.1 children per woman). With a current fertility rate of more than 5 children per woman and a predicted rate of 3.2 in 2050, Sub-Saharan Africa is the exception.

Sub-Saharan Africa would narrow the land gap by 25% and the GHG mitigation gap by 17% while decreasing hunger if it were to attain replacement-level fertility rates by 2050, along with all other areas.

It is important to take steps to achieve the three types of social progress that have caused everyone else to voluntarily lower fertility rates: expanding educational opportunities for girls, increasing access to reproductive health care, and lowering infant and child mortality so that parents don't need to have as many kids to ensure the survival of their desired number.

5. Boost grassland and livestock output.

The output of livestock per hectare varies greatly across nations and is lowest in the tropics. Since pastureland makes up two-thirds of agricultural land usage and the demand for animal-based meals is expected to increase by 70% by 2050, increasing pasture productivity is a key answer.

Between 2010 and 2050, a 25% quicker rise in the production of meat and milk per hectare of pasture may bridge the land gap by 20% and the GHG mitigation gap by 11%. Farmers may increase pasture fertilization, feed quality, and veterinary care, as well as raise better animal varieties and use rotational grazing. Governments have the power to establish production goals and provide farmers with both financial and technical help.

6. Enhance plant breeding.

Future yield increases will be necessary to meet demand. About half of historical agricultural productivity increases were attributed to conventional breeding, which is the selection of best-performing crops based on genetic characteristics.

The ability to map plant genetic codes, screen for desired DNA features, purify crop strains, and switch genes on and off more quickly and more cheaply thanks to recent developments in molecular biology holds enormous potential for increased yield improvements.

Increases in governmental and private crop-breeding expenditures must be made, particularly for "orphan crops" like millet and yam, which are crucial to the area but are not exported internationally.

7. Boost water and soil management.

One-fourth of the farmland on the planet may be affected by degraded soils, particularly in the drylands of Africa. By adopting soil and water management techniques, farmers may increase agricultural yields in locations with deteriorated soils, especially in drylands and low-carbon regions.

For instance, agroforestry, or the use of trees on farms and pastures, may increase yields and aid in the regeneration of damaged land. Faidherbia albida tree-integrated test sites in Zambia produced 88–190% more corn than control sites.

Between 2010 and 2050, a 20 percent quicker rise in agriculture yields due to advancements in crop breeding, soil management, and water conservation may bridge the land gap by 16 percent and the GHG mitigation gap by 7 percent. Agroforestry, rainwater collection, and farmer-to-farmer teaching should all get more assistance from aid organizations.

Tree ownership regulations that prevent farmers from adopting agroforestry should also be changed. Programs that assist farmers in restoring the health of their soil might also be tested by agencies.

8. Increase agricultural planting on currently used farmland.

Food production may be increased without the need for additional land by planting and harvesting existing croplands more often, either by decreasing fallow land or by increasing "double cropping" (growing two crops in a field in the same year).

The land gap would be reduced by 14 percent and the GHG mitigation gap by 6 percent if yearly agricultural intensity increased by 5 percent over the baseline of 87 percent in 2050.

To establish where cropping intensity increases are most practical, researchers should do more spatially explicit studies that take into account water, emissions, and other environmental restrictions.

9. Convert to the climatic change.

According to the 2014 Intergovernmental Panel on Climate Change study, food yields would likely drop globally without adaptation by at least 5% by 2050 and much more by 2100. For instance, it is anticipated that by 2100, growing seasons would be more than 20% shorter in areas of sub-Saharan Africa.

Crop yields falling by 10% would result in a 45 percent rise in the land gap. Implementing additional menu items, developing crops to withstand higher temperatures, setting up water conservation systems, and altering production methods where significant climate change would make it difficult to cultivate particular crops are all necessary components of adaptation.

10. Connect increased production to the preservation of natural ecosystems.

While increasing agricultural output may help conserve forests and savannas on a global scale, it can also, in certain situations, result in greater localized land destruction. Productivity increases must be connected with initiatives to stop the conversion of natural ecosystems to agriculture to prevent these outcomes.

Governments, banks, and others might, as Brazil has done, attach low-interest lending to the preservation of forests and guarantee that infrastructure developments do not harm ecosystems.

11. Lower emissions by managing manure better.

In 2010, around 9% of emissions from agricultural output came from "managed" manure, which came from confined livestock. Emissions may be significantly reduced by improving manure management via improved liquid-solid separation, methane capture, and other techniques.

For instance, utilizing highly advanced methods to nearly eliminate pollution from American pig farms would only result in a 2% rise in pork prices while lowering GHG emissions and producing several positive effects on water quality, health, and pollution.

Governments may take action by regulating agriculture, offering competitive financing for technological advancement, and setting up monitoring systems to find and fix digester leaks, among other things.

12. Lower manure-on-pasture emissions.

When animal waste and urine are dumped in fields, they produce nitrous oxide, a powerful greenhouse gas. In 2010, emissions from agricultural output were 12 percent attributable to this uncontrolled manure. New strategies include cultivating grasses that naturally stop this process from occurring as well as using chemicals to stop nitrogen from converting into nitrous oxide.

Governments may encourage farmers to use these chemical and biological nitrification inhibitors by increasing funding for research into them.

13. Lower fertilizer emissions by improving nitrogen usage effectiveness.

In 2010, emissions from agricultural output were comprised of around 19% emissions from fertilizers. More than half of the nitrogen added as fertilizer is either lost as runoff or exhaled into the atmosphere by crops. Enhancing fertilizers and their management—or the composition of the fertilizers themselves—will raise the rate of nitrogen absorption and hence decrease the quantity of fertilizer required to boost nitrogen usage efficiency, the percentage of applied nitrogen absorbed by crops.

Governments may take several actions, such as removing subsidies from fertilizers to stimulate greater nitrogen usage efficiency, establishing regulatory objectives for fertilizer manufacturers to create superior fertilizers, and sponsoring demonstration programs that do the same.

14. Use rice cultivars and management techniques that reduce emissions.

In 2010, emissions from agricultural output, predominantly methane, were at least 10% attributable to rice fields. However, there are ways to produce rice that use fewer resources and emit fewer emissions. For instance, reducing water levels during field floods may slow the development of microorganisms that produce methane.

In certain fields, this approach may increase rice harvests and save water while reducing emissions by up to 90%. Additionally, certain types of rice produce less methane. Conducting engineering evaluations to find viable prospects for lowering water levels, encouraging farmers who use water-efficient farming methods, investing in breeding projects to switch to lower-methane rice types, and increasing rice yields are all actions that need to be taken.

15. Increase energy efficiency in agriculture and switch to non-fossil fuels.

In 2010, 24 percent of the emissions from agricultural output came from the use of fossil fuels. The fundamental potential includes converting to solar and wind energy and improving energy efficiency, both of which have hardly been investigated in agricultural contexts. The gap in GHG reduction would be closed by 8% if emissions were reduced by 75% for every unit of energy utilized. There are steps to be taken, such as incorporating efficiency and low-carbon energy programs into agricultural programs and using renewable energy in the production of nitrogen fertilizer.

16. Put practical carbon sequestration strategies into practice.

The main strategy for reducing agricultural emissions has been to trap carbon in soils, but new research indicates that this is more difficult to do than previously believed. When evaluated at deeper soil levels, techniques to raise carbon, such as no-till farming, generated little to no carbon gains.

Important strategies include preventing further soil carbon loss by stopping the conversion of forests, protecting or increasing soil carbon by increasing the productivity of grasslands and croplands, increasing agroforestry, and coming up with novel ways to build carbon in areas where soil fertility is crucial for food security.

Toward a Future of Sustainable Food

People underestimate how difficult it will be to sustainably feed 10 billion people by 2050. To address the gaps in food, land, and GHG reduction, the globe must execute these menu items.
The good news is that each of them will reduce the gaps and benefit agriculture, society, and human health in addition. It will take a herculean effort, as well as significant adjustments to the way we produce and consume food. So let's start by placing all of the menu's orders!

www.ingramcontent.com/pod-product-compliance
Lightning Source LLC
Chambersburg PA
CBHW050035260726
48658CB00005B/1613